Selected Poetry of Mukaghali

Metropolitan Classics

The book "Poetry of Mukaghali" by the outstanding Kazakh writer Mukaghali Makataev is the first book of a collection of the books of classic Kazakh writers in English which the Kazakh PEN-club has decided to publish in the USA. The book collection "We Are Kazakhs" is being published under the supervision of the President of Kazakh PEN-club

Mr. BIGELDY GABDULLIN

POETRY

OF

MUKAGHALI

Translated from Russian by
Marina Vladi Kartseva

Selected Poetry of Mukaghali
All Rights Reserved.
Copyright © 2016 Mukaghali, translated by Marina Kartseva
v1.0

Cover Photo © 2016 www.shutterstock.com. Author Photo - from Mukaghali family archives. All rights reserved - used with permission.

This book may not be reproduced, transmitted, or stored in whole or in part by any means, including graphic, electronic, or mechanical without the express written consent of the publisher except in the case of brief quotations embodied in critical articles and reviews.

Metropolitan Classics

ISBN: 978-1-57480-000-5

PRINTED IN THE UNITED STATES OF AMERICA

ACKNOWLEDGEMENTS

The Publishers would like to thank the Kazakh PEN-club for their permanent support and attention to this project. Initially, it was but an ambitious idea of the Kazakh PEN-club President, **Mr. Gabdullin**, to allow for the best works of Kazakh classic writers be known globally, by way of their translation into English. Step by step, due to the tireless efforts of **Mr. Gabdullin**, the project received the financial and logistical support from influential Kazakh state organizations and private companies. The translation of this book was possible due to generous support of the "Akimat (Government) of Almaty Oblast" (Region) with the center in Taldykurgan, in Kazakhstan.

We also would like to thank the Ambassador of Kazakhstan in the USA and the Representative of Kazakhstan to the United Nations for their support of this project.

"Solitude is the destiny of a poet..."

Fate and History bow to unbending fortitude throughout the ages. Time puts everything it its place. Now and then, thinking about the past, I envision the steps leading upward. They are the steps of Time. Now and then, thinking about the poets of the older generation who have already left this world, I envision unassailable summits that tower proudly. I also envisions them climbing to those summits just as they did when they lived among us. Sometimes they look down at us from there...

They say that "you cannot sail too far in the boat of the past", but as we are looking back at the past, we sometimes notice the features of our days and those of the days to come in it. Even though he passed away almost forty years ago, I sometimes clearly see his imposing figure, his handsome glowing face, and the intent look of his eyes. This tender warm image is very close to my heart. His strong and clear voice often rings in my ears. And again, I hear his words as if coming from far away, the very words he spoke after he heard my poems and brought me to his place where the snow-white plaster bust of great Abai was standing on the desk in the corner of the room plunged into semi-darkness. Those were the days when he felt the first symptoms of his grave illness. That's why his face was sad and worried. That's how I remember him. Today he looks at us from granite pedestals, from portraits in libraries and schools places alongside the images of the great sons of the Kazakh people. He is Mukaghali Makataev, a classic writer of the Kazakh literature of the XX century, the truly people's poet, a pride of the nation.

Mukaghali Makataev is one of the brightest stars of the Kazakh poetry who was not appreciated during his lifetime and who became famous after his death. His heartfelt words, seemingly simple on the surface, reveal the secrets buried deeply in the poet's soul, and they always touch his readers' hearts.

The poet calls to mercy, humanism and kindness through depiction of irreconcilable struggle between Good and Evil, Love and Hatred. He tries to protect human beings in their striving for independence. I think that the poetry by Mukaghali Makatayev who dedicated his talent to the service of such great and sacred notions as Truth, Conscience, Humanism, Mercy, Equality and Freedom and who brought them to the previously unthinkable heights rests on that humanistic basis.

Another Mukaghali's special quality is his rendition of vicissitudes of life he himself experienced. He expressed everything he had witnessed and experienced in words and ideas which after blending in his heart, mind and soul turned into bright visible images.

It is not sometimes sufficient to read and reread translations of poems by a talented poet to feel, to a full extent, his distinctive qualities. No matter how keen one's eye and how sympathetic one's soul are, it is difficult for a person who belongs to a different culture, country and nation, who, as a rule, is deprived of an opportunity to enjoy the beauty of the language of the original to feel its true depth and have a taste from the fresh stream of its poetics. I think that a reader should know a bit more about the milieu in which the poet was born and raised, should have the idea of the national mentality, the knowledge of the poet's philosophy, of his native tongue, the traditions, and of the time when he lived and created.

The Kazakhs are one of the most ancient peoples of the Central Asia. They proved themselves a deserved descendants of the Saxons and the Huns, the tribes that had become legendary. Placed between the Dragon and the Bear, experiencing pressure from China and the Russian Empire, they, like a snow leopard, defended the Great Steppes and, despite the fierce struggle on the path to independence, preserved the ancient cultural heritage and continued to develop the epic tradition and cherish poetic talent that lived in the blood (genes) of the people. The history of the Kazakh poetry, just as the history of the cities of the Great Steppes that were destroyed during the numerous invasions to rise from ashes, goes back 2000 years. The ancient Turkic inscriptions carved on rocks by author and heroes – Yallygteghin, Bilgakagan, Tonybok and Kulteghin born and raised in the Kazakh land, can be found in the Altai and on the shores of the Black Irtish. The 100-volume collection of the folklore *Babakok cozi (The Word of the Ancestors)* published in the last ten years by the publishing house "Foliant" in Astana is yet another evidence. This impressive collection, each volume of which has over 400 pages filled with a few dozen epic poems, hundreds of *dastani* and a great number of poetic tales, fairy tales and legends, *aytisi* and *terme*, as well as sayings, proverbs and riddles, is undoubtedly a great contribution to the world culture.

The poet who learned that incomparable spiritual wealth at his mother's knees was also eager to study the classical literature of the East and the West. It is well known how difficult it is to be an "actively writing" poet, to be famous after getting ahead of other poets and becoming the best of them in the country where the improvisational poetry, the ancient art of Aitys, is so well developed and where crowds of thousands of fans get together to enjoy poetic competitions. Only a true talent can succeed under such circumstances. Besides, as I have already mentioned, it is necessary to understand the time when he was born and the time when he began his literary pursuits.

Mukaghali was born in the early 1930s when dark clouds had gathered above the heads of the Kazakhs, when the country had been plunged into the demographic disaster as the result of the tyranny and thoughtless one-sided policy of the Soviets. That cruel time can be compared to the Holocaust and the Golodomor (Death from Starvation in Ukraine in 1932-33), the time defined by historians as the period of the "genocide" when over 50% of the population perished is called "the great djute" in the Kazakh land. It was the time when people, deprived of their property, cattle and land, were forced into collective farms under false pretexts and promises, when educated outstanding representatives of science and culture, the pride of the nation, were arrested under false reports to the authorities, tortured and executed. Great numbers of people were imprisoned in the GULAG camps scattered across Siberia and out native Kazakh land during a quarter of a century. Mukaghali was an involuntary witness to those crimes. His father was killed during the first years of WW2 when the boy was 10. That prematurely made him a grow-up person and left a deep scar on his mind. We all remember a scene from one of his poems that is like a photograph turned yellow in a family album in which he, a little child, is following an ox plowing soil with a wooden plow.

The young man who had always been among the people and who had tempered in the crucible of life turned into a truly national poet. Time itself prepared him for his destiny as a great poet, though it did come at a great cost, for he was always the person of high moral principles, incapable of bowing his head before those in power, nor was he able to ingratiate himself with them or attempt to remain humble.

His poems were printed in the local newspaper when he was 14. Those were the first signs of his poetry. Three of his poems were published in the collection of poems by young poets later, when he attended the Department of Philology of Kazakh State University. He entered the German department of Alma-Ata institute of foreign languages when he was 20, but after he was expelled from the institute he returned to his native village to teach Russian at the local school. In 1956, he entered the law department of Kazakh State University which he attended for one year. He was a Kazakh radio station anchor. And again he returned to his native village to work at the local school. In 1962, he moved with his family to Alma-Ata, the capital of Kazakhstan, that time for good. He moved in literary circles closely associating with his comrades-in-trade. He worked at the newspaper *Kazakh Egibieti* and the literary magazine *Zhuldyz*. He attended the High Literary Courses at Moscow Institute of Literature for a few months in 1973, but he had to return to Alma-Ata due to the family circumstances. Just an enumeration of the above facts of his life is an evidence of the future great poet's troubled, restless, swift, explosive nature. He was the person for whom it was impossible to squeeze into any conventional frames, and is just as impossible to measure by any conventional measurements. He was perpetually in search of his niche in life and literature.

The time when he began to write coincided with the "Khrushchev's Thaw" that followed Stalin's death and the exposure of the cult of personality. That time was considered progressive during that period of the Soviet history. However, the young poet whose romantic "boat" was filled with good hopes hit underwater rocks of ideology and "broke against" the rocky shores of "everyday life", refused to succumb to the pressure of the system that had put him in this situation. He could not find the way out of the crisis and he could not fight the system openly. He would have most likely been either imprisoned or put in a mental institution had he chosen to confront the system. All he could do was express his thoughts and feelings subtly - through hints, allegories and underlying themes. The personal tragedies reflected in his works are perceived by many as their own.

If every human being is a particle of the Universe, a person born to be a poet strives for mastering the mysteries of Being in all its manifestations. He reflected about complex relations between Nature and Man, about the vicissitudes of life, about joy and sorrow, bold dreams and the bitterness of failure. The land where Mukaghali was born and raised, was filled with proudly towering impregnable mountains that challenge the sky, deep bottomless lakes, vast steppes covered with sagebrush that stretch far beyond the horizon. He sang praise to the beauty of its nature. He depicted its movement forward in time and space. Pride and generosity, the distinct features of the Kazakh national character, resonated within his works.

When he found himself in Alma-Ata in the midst of the bustling cultural life, surrounded by outstanding figures of literature and art who were the pride and glory of the nation, the young poet who published two collections of poems every year, did not shoot forward pushing his way through the literary crowd, but he definitely did not remain in the shadows as many other young poets of his generation. His unique voice got stronger with time, new facets of his natural talent sparkled, his distinctive creative qualities became more pronounced.

His works were different from those by young poets of his generation for they did not fit within the framework of socialist realism. He often demonstrated bold rebelliousness in his poems and deeds trying to break away from restrictions imposed by laws and censorship. He refused to yield to the official power, to its strict limitations and social foundations. He managed to express this inner protest in his works. The poet worried about the future of his people, and finally broke away from the influence of the communist hypnosis, after he realized his country was not free within the USSR - its position deplorable, the future of its alliance, uncertain.

Some literary historians comment, that the themes of freedom and striving for independence appeared in Mukaghali's poetry more often over the years and that some of his poems were in tune with the ideas of the December events that took place in Alma-Ata ten years after his death.

In 1969, the Board of the Writers' Union of Kazakhstan passed a special resolution brought about by the publication of Mukaghali's poems in the newspaper *Kazakh Adebieti* (06/14/1969). Intended to censor, the accusation read: "The published poems carry quite a few obscure vague ideas, mysterious and grim lines filled with underlying themes. The poet, in his attempt to reflect life with all its diversity and to depict fates of different individual people, succumbs to pessimism not typical for the majority of our people and propagates decadent sentiments." The editorial board of the newspaper that "had failed to see the ideological flaws in the poems" was strictly reprimanded for its irresponsible actions. The board was ordered to take measures against those directly responsible for the publication. In the 1930s, that would have been enough to exile the poet to Siberia. The poet experienced a time of dread – unable to work, his poems were remained unpublished, and stripped him of any means to survive. Eventually, they simply pretended he did not exist. The decision of Soviet censorship was a heavy blow for this proud person, possessing a tender, sensitive soul.

However, the ordeals of the rebellious poet who oftentimes worked against the grain, were not over. He was constantly subjected to unfair criticism in print and at literary meetings, and this too was a cause for his sufferings. The attacks resulted in his expulsion from the Writers' Union of the USSR. At that time, the poet left without royalties or the possibility to earn money to care for his 5 children. Naturally, it was not safe to express his thoughts either openly or even in the allegorical form.

During that difficult time when the doors of publishing houses were closed to Mukaghali, his knowledge of foreign literature and the history of the West and the East (which he had ardently studied for many years) helped him to get out of this impasse. As he continued to write poetry, he also dedicated his overwhelming creative energy to the translation of poetry. Three books of his poetic translations were published during his lifetime – *Leaves of the Grass* by Walt Whitman (1969), *Sonnets* by William Shakespeare, and *Inferno* (from *The Divine Comedy*) by Dante Alighieri (1971). Additionally, he translated poems by Robert Burns, Alexander Pushkin, Nikolai Nekrasov, Alexander Blok, and other poets. Some literary historians have expressed the opinion that "if Makataev didn't write a single poetic line, his translations of poetry alone would be sufficient to secure an important role for him in the history of Kazakh literature."

His translations of the works of great classical poets into his native tongue made it possible for our people to be exposed to the priceless treasures of world literature. He added the brilliant masterpieces that he himself penned, to the treasury of the golden reserve of world literature. He fulfilled yet another of his filial duties to his nation and raised his own poetry to the heights of the classics.

Unlike his young contemporaries, Mukaghali began his literary career rather late, when he was already over 30. However, in the last 14-15 years of his life, he was in the state of constant creative exploration, working with immense perseverance and passion. Even though he lived in poverty and did not have the means for a timely treatment of his grave disease, he was still able to leave us an extensive, priceless heritage – over 700 short and long poems. He reflected upon the meaning of life and the spiritual sufferings of human beings. He sang praises to courage, beauty, love and friendship. It is possible to state that there are almost no random, superfluous words, inferior combinations of words, listless, inaccurate, bad rhymes in his poetry. Every stanza, each of his poems is like flowing, seething magma which bursts and bubbles with the magical might of his talent. Such an unrestrained vibrancy reminds one of a galloping wild horse. His feelings and thoughts electrify – striking your soul, like lightning.

The Eagle on the flag of Kazakhstan is the symbol of independence, the embodiment of the proud spirit of Freedom. When Mukaghali wrote about freedom in his early poems, it is no coincidence that for its embodiment he chose the image of this proud bird. In his poem "Farewell, Eagles" (a tribute to cosmonauts) – he writes the following lines:

Oh Freedom!
You were my loftiest dream!
Give me the wings of the eagle.
Where has he flown, my white winged
Incomparable friend,
The eagle, a favorite of Freedom?
I've learned from eagles to be free.
I've developed a passion for freedom.
...Shall I stay on this obscure hill forever,
Haunted by the age-old questions?

Soon, Time would present an answer to the poet's question. The system collapsed. Our country became liberated.

Requiem Mozart, Zhan azasi was written during the last years of the poet's life that, to some extent, echoes the creations of Pushkin and Rilke, and is a very special work in a philosophic and psychological sense. In each of the four parts of the poem – *The Voices of Widows, The Voice of the People, The Voices of Orphans,* and *The Lullaby*, the author speaks on behalf of the Grave-Death, the People-the Society, the Widow-Mother and the Earth-Lullaby, and the text is brimming with profound philosophic reflections. By addressing the fate of the great composer, the poet discloses his thoughts on mortality, fickle and passing happiness, and the inconsistency of time in tune with the hopes and sorrows of mankind.

When he died at the age of 44, after succumbing to a grave illness in 1976, it is realistic to say, without any exaggeration, that the entire Kazakh nation mourned him, having realized the caliber of poet they had lost. Following his death, the name of Mukaghali has been lavished with respect and admiration. At the very end of the last century, he was named the national poet of Kazakhstan of the XX century. The poet who was not honored with awards and regalia during his lifetime, was posthumously awarded the State Prize. His 60th, 70th and 80th anniversaries were commemorated all over the country. Monuments were erected, and schools, streets and museums continue to be named after him in numerous towns and villages. Literary awards continue, too. Today, a literary magazine *Mukaghali* is published bi-monthly, and all the newspapers and magazines that refused to print his works in the past, now address his creative heritage. Readings of his works are held in high schools and colleges. Poetic tournaments dedicated to him and competitions of artistic reciting of his poems are held out all over the country. Composers pair his poems with music. Concerts that gather multi-thousand audiences are held in big cities. Everyone, young and old, know his poems by heart.

Recently, I placed two portraits on Facebook – that of Mukaghali, and that of Tupak Amaru II, the leader of the uprising of the Native Americans against the Spaniards in the XVIII century – also a national poet and hero. All who have seen the portraits emphasized their amazing likeness in their comments - not just the posture and the features of their faces, but also their stormy, inner worlds. Someone wrote - "one is the spitting image of another." Coincidentally, they died at approximately the same age.

"A poet is the messenger of his land," Mukaghali once said. I agree with his every word. His poems reflect the living language of his people. His country, his land, its language, its soul are judged by his poems. He once wrote "Speak my language, Mozart!" Time has come when his poems will be rendered in the language of Shakespeare and Whitman. Soon, the day will come when his poems will resound in the language of Dante.

Next year will be the 40th anniversary of Mukaghali's passing. With each new year that goes by, we ever more acutely feel the vitality of his poetry, and begin to better understand the true caliber of his personality. Every year, dozens of young poets dedicated their heartfelt poems to him. They address him as if he were alive...

Forty years have passed, and his poems have generated a nourishing spiritual spring for the new generations. It is without a doubt that many souls will relieve their spiritual thirst with the clean, crystalline waters of his poetic brilliance. Idols never truly die.

Ulykbek Esdaulet

About the author of the foreword:
Ulykbek Esdaulet, born in 1954, is a poet, essayist and a literary translator. He is a recipient of the State Prize, a Merited Artist of Kazakhstan and the editor -in-chief of the magazine *Zhuldyz*.

Translated by Regina Kozakov

TABLE OF CONTENTS

Oh, born yet 19
LET US LIVE, EVER CHANGING 20
MOZART - "REQUIEM 22
I. VOICE OF THE DEPARTED 24
II. VOICE OF THE PEOPLE 26
III. THE VOICES OF WIDOWS 27
IV. VOICES OF ORPHANS 29
V. A LULLABY 31
LOVE'S (INTERNAL) DIALOGUE 33
FATHER 34
THREE JOYS 35
Oh, cacophonous, restless spring 36
You – I thought were my soul's melody, sky's gold sun 37
From this black, jet-black mysterious wonder 38
Life is like ice in a rink – rolled out, steamed, smoothed 39
I am fond of you 40
If you do good 41
OH, MY ARDUOUS CROSSING!
I. Oh, my land, so free! 42
II. Oh, my luminous life! 43
Heart – beat on, keep pulsing – brain 45
THE DAY, TODAY, IS OH SO GLOOMY 46
FOLK POEM 47
Where are your lakes, oh, motherland? 48
A EULOGY 49
ENDURE, ENDURE 51
DARLING MAY'GUL
POEM ONE – When she was born into this world 52

POEM TWO – Today, I dreamt of my daughter............................. 53

AGAIN, OF MAY'GUL 54

MY JOY, YOU'RE SO FAR AWAY... 56

MY DECLARATION 57

NO, NO DOCTOR... 58

UY'SUN BORN, WAS I 60

Oh, mutual misunderstanding between humans – 61

Oh, the years ...mirage-like you ebbed and flowed..................... 62

ONE-ROOM SHACK 63

BY THE CRADLE 64

We were children, weren't we? 65

If you want to be a friend to me... 67

THE NARROW PATH.. 68

MEETING 69

KARASAZ... 70

THE LOST PLATOON 71

THE WAR'S LAST SPRING 73

GRANDMA, YOUR CANDLE WON'T DIM 74

CHARACTER 76

KHAN TENGRI – SKY KING 77

THE WANDERING GULL... 78

When in a state of yearning 79

MY DEAREST ZHENGE... 80

TO THE WOLF 82

I feel that it is not others I fear, but myself 83

I am in love! 84

May everything remain as it will 85

A CONVERSATION WITH AYBAR 86

TO MY LIFE 87

You – are the eyes of our ancestors? 88

PUSHKIN, FAREWELL 89

ON TRUTH	91
That, over there – is the sky	92
MY GOAL	93
MY AGE	95
MY ANCESTORS, MANY THANKS TO YOU	96
I WANT TO BE LIKE MOUNTAINS	97
TO MY MUSE	98
OH, HOW SHAMEFUL	99
I write poems	101
THE MOON – IN THE SKY, AND I – ON THE EARTH	102
Where are my steeds, my pastures	103
THE GUARD	104
She'd taken the jug	105
BRIDES-TO-BE	106

The titles in capital letters belong to the author. Otherwise, the first lines of the poems were used as their titles.

Oh, born yet, oh, born yet – another true poet shall be!
A veritable poet, whose lips ooze honey and bile
Having earned their trust – the widow's confidante
Compels tears to pour forth from executioner's eyes.
Oh, born yet, oh, born yet – another true poet shall be!

When the sounds of his songs, like lightning shall strike,
They'll flash, and this in the heavens, will be understood.
For the mute shall speak; the deaf shall hear,
And insight and vision to those who were blind, shall see.

LET US LIVE, EVER CHANGING…

Green leaves – heart-beat, youthful budding birch!
Oughtn't we switch lives (souls n' essence, too?)
If you transform into a human state,
I'll then start changing into birch form.
Will you agree to this, youthful birch?

(Perhaps to some, this might seem strange.)
Grant me but once the chance to live as thee!
And you'll have your chance at this hectic world,
With human eyes, but once to glance.

Now, as birch, I'll too, observe
My own place. I'll find in forest depths,
Upon this strange and unfamiliar life,
With eyes of birch I'll gaze upon.

As you were nurtured by the earth
So, was I, nurtured by her, too.
As someone had begotten you,
So, indeed, had someone begotten me.
No voice you have, budding birch.
Yet your own soul, you do still own!
But I'm a man, and you've been sown.

Everything that I, myself, possess – is heart.
Yet – you've been given a myriad hearts,
'Tis why your life's years seem limitless –
The selfsame twin of years to come.

Everything I own is my one heart.
If it stops, forever I depart.
For if your thousand hearts do wither,
When verdant spring returns once more,
They'll soon revive, and quiver!

Green leaves, heart-beat, youthful budding birch!
Oughtn't we switch lives?
Having become human, you'll walk with confidence!
Having become a birch, I'll stand with confidence!
Oughtn't we just try? Take a risk – switch lives!

And so, life I'll go on living,
To our mother earth, so tight, I clutch,
Sometimes - I'm human, sometimes – a birch,
And so, we'll live – ever changing!

MOZART - "REQUIEM"

Someone had come, enveloped in clothing black.
"Compose for me a requiem, Mozart!"
And vanished, as quick as he'd come.
Was it, perchance, a phantom seen?
Or had it but a person been?
In mournful vestments veiled was he – begrieved, it'd seem.
Was it cruel fate who'd robbed him of his family?
Mozart – vexed, distressed,
Cast aside at once his work, did he.

His name (and who was he?) was all he wished to gain.
And so - he threw himself in chase,
And stood outside awhile, waiting, just in case.
For both the stranger's name, his origin – still obscured
Damn it! The cloaked figure did – suddenly – vanish.

"Compose for me a requiem, Mozart!"
The mournful voice bespoke.
The requiem's melody all his thoughts consumed
That agony, and cruelty – in this life us surely binds.

We must – instantly, entirely – all these thoughts, renounce.
"I shall write it...I shall!" he then announced.
Was I awake?
Or was this dreamt?
Oh, Heavens, glorious!
Then upon the keys his hands had played – lovingly caressed.

"Farewell, farewell – my brother beloved, farewell!"

As though a voice with sorrow, heavily did sigh.

"Oh, Mozart, farewell!" it vocalized.

Was it, perhaps my heart that to me, thusly cried?

Some moments passed, his face's color drained.

"Oh, compose for me a requiem, Mozart!"

Could it be angels, even fey?

Then, once again – through his hands, the melody did flow

Inconsolable, shared with each voice his despair

Life then swelled – with this heavy voice, so sorrowful.

With compassion and thoughtful care – life and death spoke of matters private.

I. VOICE OF THE DEPARTED

'Twas you I loved,
With full heart and soul, I loved – Oh, Luminous World!
Forevermore, I'll love – even if hell's deep abyss must I occupy,
Perhaps, caressing me – your ray, immaculate,
Oh, Luminous World!
Could then gently halt –
Arrest itself, right upon my tomb's lid, this grim chest!

From heavens' farthest reaches – for us all, your light did shine.
Not only had I felt it – but, indeed, I knew it, too.
For me, it'll all cease – in a moment, a flash, instantaneously.
Do not desert me,
Do not leave my side, oh, Luminous One!
May your brilliant ray pour down, showering me –
Even if my existence be but grass jutting through – this I'll do!

All but satisfied, for everything, my soul did thirst.
In life, I'd experienced so much, so many concerns!
And my life's lived out.
So much joy lived through – and all this,
(As it just so happens) isn't worthy of
Your Ray – *Evanescence* – to which nothing can compare.

Oh, Ephemeral Ray...
Oh, Temporal, Luminous Temple of mine!
How will I – to such darkness (this prison!) retire?
Express this in words, I've discovered, I know not how.
Go ask the dead, I'd like to say,
What meaning this life of ours does possess
To the souls with firm hold of life's breath, still preserved.

Whilst alive, we didn't appreciate (nor its meaning quite grasp)
That, which they call "Life".
For – excepting that gleaming ray – all is futility
And the rest - pitiful.
It's all so frenetic, frenzied and foreign.
That which they call Light – oh, that temporal Light!
Like for precious droplets of rain– for this Light – I thirsted still!
And if this be life – I've quite had my fill.
Live forevermore!
Live forevermore!
Oh, Luminous World!
And I? I am no more, no more, no more…

II. VOICE OF THE PEOPLE

When the arctic frosts and storms subside – the Death's Night,
When spring arrives, with flowers blankets earth's faire guise,
And the tulips through earth's blackened crust shall thrust,
The chest has its heart incised.

When the skies shall shudder – by some divine might,
When the very heavens and land begin to quake,
Disentangling, then slashing the clouds, pitch black,
Your bright light this gloom shall pierce – and illuminate.

When the future – with a cry – into this world shall emerge,
When the present generation – the past's – replaced,
Then like bridges that hang suspended, you'll support
The connecting of hearts to each other.

We by you –
You by us – roused to inspire,
Heartened thus, your soul – its people – could then nourish
A true nomad. In this realm, you'll not retire
Upon this journey eternal you've embarked
The majestic voyage that spans th'immortal sands.
And, as this grief is a cold and bitter woe,
The people's souls creep in, claim, then chill – she won't.
Lest the people not surrender to the claws of oblivion,
Be calm, confident – have faith!
Into the pit of people's vanished memories, you'll not be thrown!

While a cruel and callous death the people can never break,
For you, their longing shall not annihilate.
If to hide your body, they decide – the earth, our mother, shall envelop you!
Though, not so it is for time, unwilling try!

III. THE VOICES OF WIDOWS

In this temporal life, all is temporal.
In this temporal life,
Is there any soul more woeful than a widow's?
When upon this temporal world,
One is left behind in solitude,
With one's dreams left unfulfilled,
Could anyone, anything change?
In this temporal life, all is temporal.
Could it be, in life (so transitory)
All's deserted - quite simply ceased,
Not endured – future sunsets to see?
Indeed, light of mine – you're finished,
Your dreams you're not destined to meet.

Walking amongst us, the noble one,
Death had come down, still slyly cloaked
The soil black – had devoured and digested
That lightning, which from the heavens did bolt.

And the widow, now defenseless,
From her hopes forever disconnected.
And the candle – burning bright,
The wind swooped down and crushed with might.

And the age-old earth, in having gobbled you up
With verdant life, countless times will leaf.
And so she'll triumph and celebrate,
But what will she, to me, bequeath?
Sorrow she will spill, with all her haste,
As hot tears shall stream down my face.

And my tomb, with heart of stone,
Will myself to stone convert.
And my corpse one day nail to the dirt.

When your beloved woods and lakes,
With the presence of birds are graced,
From the far-flung horizon's passes,
When that mournful mirage I glimpse,
Your soul, pure grief, does you bemoan,
You're filled with longing, with heart-of-woe.

How must I, this woe, endure?
Who could ever to you compare?
What must I, with death (that thief) do?
Drowning in my own pool of tears,
No one knows me, and gone, are you,
So I'll live – despondent, deformed.
From whence did this black earth first thirst
For widows' heartache and despair?

Surrounded on all sides by fog
My eagle – to that place, you've soared,
That distant realm of no return!
So fare thee well!
My dear dream, so tattered, so torn,
Farewell, my beloved! Fare thee well!

IV. THE VOICES OF ORPHANS

We are –
Orphans,
Orphans!
In February's midst,
Our feet will stand in bitter cold – frost and snow.
In this life, so greedy, we must ask for alms,
For the earth's calm – we disturb, and we alarm.
We are – orphans!
We are – orphans!
We treat this world like a ball in our palms, so small!
For we do not die easy,
Don't be annoyed with us, please!
Do not yell – no,
At us, do not yell,
Do not raise your voices!
At many a door we've implored for shelter!
If need be, over your heads – we're sure to jump!
Because, who are we? Orphans!
Don't be annoyed with us, and do not dare yell!
We are – orphans!
The world we can enter and leave at our whim.
We won't ably distinguish the fall from the spring!
And if there are people in this world filled with woe,
There will also be orphans, wherever you go.
We'll live on forever, we'll live – on and on!
We are – orphans!
We are not thieves, we are not crooks!

But how could we save face – from our cast's disgrace?
There's but one kind word that keeps warmth in our hearts,
When cursed frost with searing flames our feet lick.
Upon kind-hearted souls, harm we'll not inflict!
And, how shall we somehow find souls with hearts kind?
Yet – for the soul of an orphan, would kindness suffice?
We are – orphans!
We are – orphans!
And, as orphans, we have grown!
This earth we've knocked round-and-round, much like a ball!
From this life, we've seized peace, we've taken the calm!
In this life – one another will envy,
Whether living,
Whether dead - they are strangers to us all.
Gather 'round, all orphans, from this big, round globe,
In the name of Truth - ban together - and in the name of hope!

V. A LULLABY

Sweetly sleep,
Sweetly sleep,
Pure, darling child of mine.
Calm your head, close your eyes,
Rest, my boy, and sleep tonight,
So forever I may rock you, tight.
This timeless lullaby,
I have saved for you – my sweet child!

For here exist no days, my son.
And the sun here – knows not to rise,
To throw its rays upon dark skies.
Rest - my darling boy.
Sweetly sleep, pure child of mine!

No sadness here, nor happiness,
No ranks exist, no honor, and no fame,
No rumors my dear, shall reach here,
Nor shall ever reach, an arrow strayed!
Sweetly sleep, sweetly sleep – my sweet child, free of guilt.
Lay with peace, eternal bliss!

No wars here be, nor arguments,
No envy, lies or fights.
Many such spirits past us went.
Pure, sweet child of mine – you're not alone!

Sleep, my boy, and nothing fear.
For the family, and wife, and friends,
The sworn foe and the associate,
Will all gather here.
Sleep my boy, and nothing fear.

Hush thus, endless steppes and brush,
Do not disturb my darling boy,
For I can only lull him, sweet,
But eternity – for him will weep.
Sweetly sleep,
Sweetly sleep,
My unsullied slave of God,
Having found your peace, you rest in me.
How much respect to life you gave,
The same upon you, will death bestow.
To her chest, she'll clutch you tight, for infinity.
Sweetly sleep,
Sweetly sleep,
My innocent, child sweet…
Sweetly sleep…
Sweetly sleep…
Sweetly sleep, forevermore!

LOVE'S (INTERNAL) DIALOGUE

If, having turned into a bird – I take flight, then vanish – what would you do?
    I'd set off in search of you, if need be – eternally.
If into a fire I fall, and ignite – what then?
    Then as in ashes a phoenix resurrects, I'll walk with you.
And what if I'm blurred, like a mirage - obscured?
    Then as zephyr, I'll get wind of you, pursue you.
And what if, anguish and woe, with you I'd combine?
    Darling, hush! There's nothing I'd not endure!

FATHER

Father, I'll soon find myself older than you.
At times, I rejoice,
And at other times, I am instead – joyless.
Yet with this life, your son fell in love – it's true.

Joy hasn't left me here to stand with empty hands.
Life still lures me with pleasures onto her lands.
One lion, from this life, will depart.
Yet, the other lion – shall he still roam on like lions roam?

But mourn not, my father, for your hearth burns on.
It shall burn for eternity, knowing no calm.
For much offspring you've got, and whilst they're alive,
The honor of man and your people shall thrive.

Father, seeing the legacy that you've left,
The joy that 'pon your four grandsons' faces crept,
Then your cap, so worn, ever soaked in your sweat,
Taking turns, to ensure each, the prized relic caressed.

Then - they'd sniff, their tiny noses wrinkled in delight.
Mom sat, filled with joy, in pure bliss, praising God for this sight.
Some sort of sentiment my nerves did excite,
Rising up, in my throat like a knot, so tight.

THREE JOYS

The first thing that brings joy to my heart – my People,
To Him I'd give my thoughts' precious gold, crystal.
For if he lives on, so do I – I shan't despair.
My worth'll be greater than gold, and more rare.

The second joy in my life – the Word,
With it, stone hearts into pieces I've splintered.
Even if, at times, I've found I'm sick of life's woes,
My sacred language I would never disown.

I have yet one more, third, joy – called Motherland,
If you'd asked – what is god? The grand Motherland!
Is there a person in this world whose soul has faded?
Think not twice – hither comes, with my flame, you'll blaze..

For yourself, a family build.
You must grow, bear fruit, and with blossoms be filled,
May your grandsons and their sons multiply.
Yet – you I'll cautiously remind,
For, you may expect no kindness from me
If, instead of my flame, a bullet you seek.
Three priceless joys in the palm of my hand lie.
Life such luck did provide – hard to believe, at times!
Three suns, their rays did emanate from my sky –
To Atirau, to Arku, Alatua – and Altai!

***

Oh, cacophonous, restless spring,
When torrential rains you bring,
When your deafening lightning booms,
Splitting thunderous clouds straight through -
Think of me.

When clouds – regal, tufted – glide by,
When through summer's forest you stride,
Think of me, in your daydreams.
When you, alone, your company keep -
Think of me.

When November's time rolls around,
When gardens turn to barren ground,
Arid grass, like a wall, stands tall,
When unruly leaves the ground be-sprawl -
Think of me.

When white flakes transform earth's dull hue,
When trees don jewels of frozen dew,
When earth, dawn's pale glimmer does touch,
When February's frosts dissolve your blush,
Think of me!
Think of me!
***

***

You – I thought were my soul's melody, sky's gold sun,
You gave me flowers each time I had come.
Like lightning's embers flash across the horizon,
Couldn't you just reveal yourself to me, but once?

Back then - I'd have disappeared, with clouds suffused
With lightning. I'd have attempted a duel.
I'd have swum at your heels, to white clouds transformed.
If but once, had peeked through – my young, boyish love.

Oh, sweet zephyr! From hills, chasms - scents, gently you drift.
How to you my pond'ring thoughts seem to constantly shift.
Wondering, how you must now live,
My seraph – clearer than water, whiter than milk!

Melancholy, I battle, that thirsts to drain me,
My youthful days, one by one, all flee.
Show thyself – but once, I'll calm – no more grieve,
Wherefore are you, where – my young boyish love?
***

***

From this black, jet-black mysterious wonder,
From true black hue, run not asunder!
Sleep enjoyed, pure-white, like babe's cheeks
To be woken by that pitch-black night.

This black, jet black night - I'd survived
Greeting lucid, bright dawn when it'd arrived
Without black's darkness, I suppose
The true worth of light – I'd never know.

My love's locks are blacker than night,
Her eyes comprised of jet-black light.
Gaze thus - her complexion, snow-white,
Hence, her magnificence brings such delight!

Cream with coal – interchange, rearrange,
Forever to be interlaced.
If white I'd decided to grab,
So why not then black, also nab?

There's one girl with eyes black, pitch-black
From the true black hue – do not run far!
In the heavens glisten many stars,
Who in black, pitch-black night all spark.
***

***

Life is like ice in a rink – rolled out, steamed, smoothed.
If poems I'm to verse, I must first weep anew.
If the finish line ribbon I'll break right through,
Even God's strength won't, my own, outdo.

That grief and woe – I'll then banish, cast right out.
Sorrow – that bitch, her eyes I'll gouge, this I vow.
Guessing from whence that woe-thief will creep to spring,
I'll hide in wait – to a troubled doe, akin.

Up life's steps I march with vigor – boldly, I go,
I'm one to run around pitfalls they call - woe.
If tears – whole seas, I'd spill - would it dim the flame
Ablaze within – still chained, yet craves to break.

No! No longer will I dim, convince or weep.
Not happiness dwells near the living, but grief.
For life's river – she will not stir.
From the tears one helpless man's grief would create.

No - I'll walk not so, ever-loaded with life's woe.
If a man trips – he'll not dip. Straight down he'll go.
Rather than joy, split up into little bits,
Better my woe, which, when alone, compels me to think.
***

***

I am fond of you.
And yet –
From you – I've endured more than from any before.
You, I'll forewarn – blame yourself. It'll be your guilt
If one day you've discovered – I've disappeared, quit.

From you – I've endured more than from any before,
So that you'd elevate. Myself, I did deprecate.
Who had me bewitched, by you made?
Oh, dear God!
How did I let it, to this point, escalate?

Who had me bewitched, by you made?
(Without you, joy, laughter will still permeate.)
Who was it?
Who, to spin circles 'round you, did me persuade
And chased, like a circus horse made to degrade?

Doing all that you'd asked,
Without thinking through actions, I do not act.
'Tis but to you, my will, I do submit,
Obediently to you, my head does wilt.
Oh how unnatural, unlike me, this is!

I am fond of you.
Yet, yet…
Why must your kindness with my tears wet, be met?
That which I'd said, that I'm fond of you, isn't true.
My heart's shredded, into pieces, because of you.
***

***

If you do good,
>   Do not say, I must repay,
>   My pet!
 If your gift's given as debt,
>   Then without your gold, I'll be set.
Having become oxen to you,
>   In my life's remaining days, I refuse to
Lug this weight around, that due to you I'd accrued.

Having nourished me with her milk,
>   My mother never uttered – one day, you'll pay!
I still feel the weight of my debt,
>   To my father, not repaid – on my back, heavy, it weighs.
Not once expecting a cent back,
>   Oh, so many friends supported me – a whole pack!
And return it – I always wanted to,
>   But what should I do?
>   I never did get any richer.

To my people, forever,
>   How long (God only knows), I've owed up to my elbows,
When will I repay?
>   What choice do I have – what to say?
>   From this I cannot deviate, I cannot stray.
I was born indebted.
>   To this earth, so merciful.
Which doesn't say or know what I owe?

I do now whine about how I'm fined
>   For your favors or actions kind.
For I'll not be able to return it,
>   And who knows, when I'll strike it rich.
For I'm that fellow,
>   The only foal of the destitute, penniless beggar's,
On whose tether the pressure shan't release, not ever!
***

OH, MY ARDUOUS CROSSING!

I.
Oh, my land, so free!
Two chances to live, there won't be
(At least with death, twice, we won't plead.)
Tomorrow, from you, I shall flee.
Swan-like, wishing not to diffuse
In the aqueous, crystalline mirror.
One time I revolve, and disappear.
I'd cool off, I'd warm up,
Dashing, and falling, at times,
At least by twenty-five, I'd realized
What is was to be sixteen.
Oh, my land, so free!

Oh, youth – you were a young man's promise!
And you were his solace, his goddess.
Bright burning flame, never plunging into darkness,
How many souls having warmed?
How many souls having burned?!
Tire not, my dear.
A day away is fifty, so near!
Life's blossoming, youth's melodies,
How many hurdles we've overcome,
Or times through the snowstorms we walked, numb.
It's a miracle, that from all this, yet again, we've sprung!
Even back then – prose, we'd composed,
Heart-to-heart our feelings disclosed.
Eighteen and thirty years old,
Divided down the middle, as twins we posed.
Through how many winters lived – bitter and grim,
How many times had we pined for spring?
You and I - the people's favorite sweethearts.
Yet, we never became madmen.

Choosing the tallest mountains,
Facing those difficulties, we walked on again.
For a man of courage, such is the fate,
Upon the field of battle, many challenges face.
How many young men simply erased?
We could always be found there in our youth,
The village they called Truth.
Such immense challenges we had to bear,
And though our backs right down to the bone it did wear
The brunt of it, our bond, never did tear.
To each other we were, as brothers,
And so together, we despaired.
In those homes, where the hearth had grown cold,
You and I – a blazing fire, we did glow.
And in love, we always believed
In love's haze, falling, genuinely.
And, in our village – always with its *bayan*
Like the *kozi*, we'd roll in – bravely.
Foolish, we never did become,
We mastered being sweethearts of the Nation.

II.

Oh, my luminous life!
My youth, so crystal-clear to me now,
Oh, so timid and shy, was I – like a girl!
And your hair a flowing, silken swirl,
And your braid hung to the very floor,
What shores do you roam, girl whom I adore?
But, no matter, for wherever you've explored,
Whenever spring's wings unravel to soar,
Rejoice, my darling, rejoice!
Oh, my radiant, sun-laden spring,
Sweet spring – your priceless bygone memories still sing.
Oh, my arduous crossing!

How did I, you, so effortlessly traverse?
How did I emerge victorious?
Nor noticed how I'd reached forty years of age!
Had I thought, but once, that I'd abandon one day
The cool of shaded gardens that the steep hillsides did carpet?

Oh, my arduous crossing!
So many joys I have,
So many regrets from the past!
That dress – calico
Around your waist tucked and fitted just so.
The way the wind your skirt did gently sway,
How upon your chest, two small strawberries lay,
Who'd known, the dove, from your side never having strayed
Would unexpectedly, from us, fly away?
Even your sister had been there that day,
How, and to what distant lands had you fluttered away?
Yet, wherever you wander,
May her home be blissful.
May it be blissful.
May her home –
Not a prison be – nor a cage enclose.
All in all, may she shed not a tear.
May she live never knowing grief or fear,
Since over another threshold you've veered,
(For eternity, my darling, to you I'll be near!)
For every single time spring does arrive,
You'll give roots and within me – be alive.
The unopened bud of the saffron rests,
Harvesting, gaining strength in my chest.
When you feel spring's warmth into the atmosphere swim,
Having split my grave in two, you'll burst through – and yet again, you'll sing!
Oh, my arduous crossing!

***

Heart – beat on, keep pulsing – brain,
Keep on spilling and pumping through my veins, blood!
I've yet to serenade life with songs of love.
Oh, sweet Muse!
Only before you shall I bow.
Hither come quickly, come to me now
To distant lands I'm rushing, lands unbound.

Life – with my love songs, I will serenade,
Unheard, unseen – to this very day.
My heavy rains hang suspended, in heavens above
My garden's fruits, from their branches, have yet to plunge,
Abandon I shan't, 'til nothing of mine remains.

Oh, how bitterly cold is death,
First shrouded, then – in this icy grave placed.
Into this life, I arrived with faith,
If I'm to leave, without faith I'll not be erased
May the person be cursed, who attempts to chain down
The art of language - of captivating words and sounds.

Without moment's thought, all of life I'd renounce,
If from language, words such as alabaster
And dagger would, abruptly, vanish.
I've yet to serenade life with love ballads.
When am I to sing, and when – my lips fasten?!
(Before you I come, and I bow in despair.)
Must my dreams to sing, I truly abandon,
Oh, sweet Muse!
To distant lands I'm rushing, lands untraveled.
***

THE DAY, TODAY, IS, OH, SO GLOOMY

The day, today, is so gloomy,
And unwilling, his face's gaze, to illuminate.

The grey fog's swirls loom, village consume, and beyond –
Could it be, indeed – for me, someone waits,
With a face – in the same gloom, encased?

Who shall remain, linger – myself there to seek?
All the while, love did wait for me, to greet
Yes, clearly I see - she's lost faith, too long did she anticipate,
'Tis she, it appears, is this gloomy day.

Today, grandmothers or fathers I have not.
Who'll wait for me - no one's blessings to be sought.
Who would then sow, my soul's deeply-rooted woe,
Who needs the ranks, honor or glory I've got?

Status, title, name?
From where could these be obtained?
My cheerful existence has all but ended.
On the hilltop lies my heart's true soul-mate, my one friend.
Who, always for me did wait – with smiling face.

Today, the day looms, ever-gloomy,
My mood seems glued to the weather's changing face.
No desire – spare, or your pity convey!
What more can you claim – that I to you, repay?

FOLK POEM

My dear,
I - am no Lermontov, nor Pushkin.
Nor have I told anyone I'm Esenin.
Yet, Kazakh folk poetry is my strength.
For, within, grand mysteries lie in its depths.

My eldest brother remains, to lay in lands strange,
Perhaps then, with blood – his message he did convey.

Your dignity, folk poem, I gently place in the grave.
Like the true Kazakh, you too – are plain.

From rawhide cut into even strips,
I weave a unique, never before seen whip.
If my whip you don't admire – from me, depart,
Open this plain house door, my counterpart!

Into even-even strips the stubble-field's tilled
Why not water it a bit, let it drink its fill?
If the Kazakh people's folk poem somehow dies,
How must I, dark bloody tears, for her cry?

Inquisitiveness is one of my characteristics:
I sow, grow and crossbreed wheat and millet.
My cauldron-brain will boil, until it's molten
Will separate; liberate the Kazakh folk poem.

How could I utter that I am a poet?
I simply repeat – 'twas my nation who told it.
Dressed in plain shirt – the Kazakh folk poem,
In a caftan adorned, to him I return.

***

Where are your lakes, oh, motherland?
I'll shift into a small, small fish.
Where's your mountain range, motherland?
Deer-like, I'll prance about 'n skip.

Where are your steppes, great motherland?
Lying there, I contemplate.
Where's my great-grandpa, motherland?
With that beard of his, I'll play.

Where are your deserts, motherland?
A great thirst I'll endure, (oh, such thirst)!
In barren, lifeless, arid sands
My life I'll end, so I'm cursed.

Where are your azure skies, motherland?
I'll come alive, and take flight!
Where are your winds, great motherland?
Revived I'll be, and delight!
Where are your arctic peaks, motherland?
To them I'll bow down, extol.
Have you enemies, motherland?
I'll shoot swiftly, like a bow.

***

A EULOGY

Night.
Buffet.
Hospital.
I, alone, wrestle with sleep.
I'm called by verdant mountains, steep,
Emerald forests, vast open steppes.

Poems' string, snipped
In memories, village drifts in.
Heart, now warmed.
Hearing, gentle noise of swarms
Of lambkins, billies, foals and fillies.

Poetry, suddenly
I am disclaiming.
(Who needs the heartache?)
Running from gadflies with the calf-babe,
Racing with small foals, unrestrained.

And then, the lush garden calls,
Dispersing and scattering thoughts
In ev'ry which way.
Now, liberated from those places,
I'd love to escape – far, far away.
Make my way to a small spring,
And climb atop some hill.
Alas, albeit for me,
It's uncertain, if I shall reach,
The goals I've made, luring me.

Hospital.
Night.
Lunchroom table.
My one and only workspace,
The one, true haven.
And oh, my soul!
Beloved – where, oh, where are you?
Abandon me not, all alone!

ENDURE, ENDURE

Endure, endure!
Endure, then endure some more!
This life sure does love its sufferers.
Pearlescent, dawning sun – full of bright hope,
For someday, one day – it'll all come; it'll all unfold.

Pity not, certainly for today – don't blame.
Life, life!
We should not ourselves resign, nor her impugn,
For you're not destined to trip up, in perpetuum,
Rise up again, you've got every right to run.

I understand that your soul does surely ache,
But you've endured, so endure – simply take a break.
Listen, and choose a peaceful state,
Bow your head, yet at another's foot do not abase.

Endure, endure!
Endure, then endure some more!
Mountain stream flows, cascades down – delivering blows,
And, in defending your spotless honor, pure
Go ahead, rise against him – go fight your war.

DARLING MAY'GUL

POEM ONE
When she was born into this world - it was spring,
The earth strewn with petals, sun's gold rays did swim,
The wind's gentle wisps, her face kissed with tenderness.
What in life caused her such dreadful woe, as this?

What in life caused her such dreadful woe, as this?
For she had not been, at all, by life dismissed.
I do not grieve – these are poems of mine, unwritten,
Forcing me, needlessly, many sighs to emit.

Forcing me, needlessly, many sighs to emit…
In truth, I can't say she's dismayed by this life,
What's there to say, but – in this dog's life,
People are needlessly born, needlessly die.
Isn't it so – that hundreds come, and hundreds go?
Alright, what's there to say – are not the steppes' roses,
In springtime grown – dead and wilted, by the fall?

POEM TWO

Today, I dreamt of my daughter – fragile thing.
Little girl of mine, small crimson flower picked.
Oh, who'd it been that plucked these grapes from the vine,
With nectar, ripening, sweet in this garden of mine?

In my dreams, my daughter calls to me,
There she sits – opposite bank, by river we're split,
Forgive me, child, I cannot come. Forgive me!
I'm the biggest "dimwit" that on this earth lives.

I'm the biggest "dimwit" that on this earth lives.
Massive passes do lay before me, still.
Be patient my dear child, for where can you go,
You, on whom much black, ashen soil was thrown?!

Please do not utter – "Come to me!"
To the will of fate, for now, please submit.
One day, our two roads will merge – that were once split,
What can I do for now but grieve, sweet child – yearn, miss?

AGAIN, OF MAY'GUL

How must I rid myself of your apparition?
You appear – and always, right next me, sit.
You've died, my dear child, yet I'm still living,
I live.
I live!
I know you can see it!

My soul's made peace with both punishment and death,
Don't be upset,
I implore – no more punishment, nor distress.
If this be true – I'll see you in the realm of light,
But for now – my heart, my sweet, please, give me peace!

For I'm a living soul.
You are a vision, a ghost.
You know, it's not I who killed you.
To me, no one could surpass, nor rival you.
Yet, you are a vision, an apparition,
An apparition, you are!
Who could tear us from death?
Lay still and wait for me, in your darkened depths.
Whilst alive, in this life, I'll walk on,
For my heart's special throne, you do sit upon.

Sweet May'gul, modest flower, azure sky of mine!
Who would surrender their heart to death's demise?
You were my heart!
Yet – somehow,
You are a vision, an apparition!
Please, come no more, from my vision – depart.

***

In the mornings, ousting the cows into the pastures,
My darling little minx romped and roamed in the grove,
The sun's rays settled upon the dew in the willow's treetops, fracturing,
A myriad colors ebbed and rippled, flowing over, and bestowed an enchanting glow.

The flow of the great Karasaz – the tender sapling quivered, by the wind rippled.
I gently nudged the young sprout, fiercely flapping in the wind.
How was I to know that this young sapling, upon becoming a tree,
Was destined to kindle my heart's beating strings?

Beneath the current of the Karasaz – the young sapling, quivered by the wind, rippled.
You gently nudged the young sprout, flapping in the wind.
Back then, it was only sorrow, that my thoughts did permeate,
I supposed one day, it would come along, dispelling it all, just as I'd longed.

Together we grew, the young willow sprout and I,
Together we awoke as dawn filled the sky,
As it turned out, my fate I'd entrusted and placed,
In my palms that still felt so much, but had lost all faith.
Gently, you touched the young sprout growing in the great Karasaz,
And I touched the sprout you gently brushed with your finger.
Could I have ever guessed, that – one day that sprout,
Turning into you, would ignite in my heart, a fire throughout?

In the wee hours of the morning, I paid a visit to the grove again,
In front of me a tree stood tall, rippled by the wind.
We were twins – in the very same grove, we grew.
Why have you, my darling minx, suddenly become frightened of me?
***

MY JOY, YOU'RE SO FAR AWAY

Don't fool yourself, nor console yourself in vain.
Do not allow yourself to take flight on the deceptive wings of hope!
All just has left me, none remains,
Yet, for me, it waits – far away, this I know.

It is still unclear - shall I reach it, or not?
Or, perhaps, left alone on this endless stretch of road – my joy never to be caught?
Yet, for me, it waits far away – this I know.
Am I to grasp it, am I ever to revive – to bloom and grow?

And though I've lived so many, so many woes,
I won't ever tire of seeking my happiness, no!
Oh, dearest life – if possible, could you prolong yourself, just a bit?
For joys that are fleeting, I vow, not wish!

Oh, sweet life of mine!
I receive you in my embraces, let us intertwine!
My dream, I compare to the Volga River.
Don't trespass, nor cheat me of my happiness, far away!
I've dreamt of it, longingly – thirsting for it each day.

The years are so quick to fly by – marching off, one by one.
Summer has passed. Fall, too, is nearly gone.
Winter, also, shall pass…And with it, I too, am certainly through.
Just as long as that joy's fateful search for me, yet again, will renew.

MY DECLARATION

It's my birthday today!
Can you believe it?
Why are those people not celebrating it?
I would've thrown quite the shindig myself,
But, alas, the Almighty himself,
Decided not to bless me with an overabundance of wealth.

Why is the world so silent, so speechless,
Instead of blowing on the coal embers, until they glow red-hot again?
Why won't they throw flowers, in handfuls, or bowers
Or say: "Here's your coat;
Here's your horse; saddle her up, and go!"

Or, maybe, these people dislike something that sleeps deep within me,
That my life I've lived in vain, thrown away needlessly?
Oh, my dear people!
I was convinced I understood your dignified ways and virtues,
Could it truly be, my life's gone by, with no purpose? All of it in futility?

Well, if they don't want to celebrate with me, then so it shall be.
What on earth am I to do it about it, anyway?
So it seems no festivities shall I see, no gifts or celebrations for me.
And so, my dearest missus, hand me my pen and my inks.
My declaration I'll write now, to the Future pass down, and take my bow in parting.

NO, NO, DOCTOR

Constantly, I'd find myself winding more and more weight to my heart.

Poor little thing! It seems I've tired you till the end, my dear, you must be scarred!

Were you deceptively poisoned…perhaps you were dragged through the mud?

Or was it in some other way, that on you, they tried to prey?

But the truth of it lays in this – my heart is ill, never ceases to ache.

Oh, doctor, doctor!

Am I meant to shoulder this burden all my life?

Why was I the only one chosen, to suffer the ill fate of such strife?

And why are you looking at me, with pity pouring out of your eyes?

Tell me, tell me, doctor! Tell me the whole, death-dealing truth.

There's no sense in dancing around it, so out, enough with this ruse!

Am I destined to be thrown from the path of life early, no longer to roam?

Why not just tell me the truth, freely,

Instead of talking in circles, equivocally?

I feel like a fool – God's helpless little slave,

Cloudy blood, like thick mud runs through my veins.

I'm at a loss. How have I wronged you, heart?

What did I give to him insufficiently, what could I bestow – that he doesn't already own?

The blood in me is beginning to boil, yes, it's boiling in me!

Quick, do something, doctor!

To my health and well-being could you proceed to give some thought?

Do not permit Death's grip to be laid upon the poet,

To be ferried with him, to an alternate realm!

No…no, goodness, no!

No, no, doctor, never!
Do not consider implanting some other heart into me.
I have no desire to envision a foreign sound, or a foreign beat.
How am I to tell people, that my doctor (rather insensibly) means
To secretly pry me open, and grab my heart, without me knowing?

In which direction, should I take off, with a pocketed foreign heart?
This stranger's life – how could I exploit it, or adopt it?
Why, thank you for the present, my charitable fellow!
Although, I know no heart would ever suit me better than my own!

Switch?!
Did you just say – I'll switch?!
Yet, most likely, my star would not shine as brightly after this!
Having buried my own distinct and singular heart,
In the life of another, could I move onward, as if it were just a fresh start?
Come now, heart, kick it up a notch!
What regrets have I truly got?
Ah, but of course…
…my very own heart, born of the eternal life source, how could it not perish?

No, no, doctor!
No, doctor, no!
Don't touch my heart. It's for the best.
So let it beat on – each heart in its native chest!

UY'SUN BORN, WAS I.

I am Uy'sun. Deem me water-bearer, I will bear water.

I'm not accustomed to blood spilling, nor with the task of conquering lands.

Hey, brothers! Come visit our mountains, looming high

No enemies here will hide, no quarrels exist, just silence and peace of mind!

I am – Uy'sun. Call me a shepherd, and I will herd sheep.

And I see nothing wrong with minding the kettle, either.

I am – Uy'sun, I am of the Elder Zhuz, I have seniority!

I say "Elder" – but you'll not catch me imposing seniority!

In fact, I am smaller than the middle and youngest,

Having said "Elder" – I've made certain not to pressure them.

If our people are to face the dawn of a difficult juncture,

I will be the pointed head of the spear of my two younger brothers.

Uy'sun – I am, call me Elder, and Elder I shall be.

I'm slave to humility, and to the respect of the Elderly.

With my two younger brothers I am most eager to share my inheritance,

If, to me, they shall gallop over - with wind-whipped hair, helmetless.

***

Oh, mutual misunderstanding between humans – what utter torture!
Sensible youth, you've understood this truth – thank you! Thank you!
You are young, and oh, so full of fire!
Full of fire, and bursting with energy!

You, the sensible youth!
Poetry – is my life, my breath,
My choicest words for my pure-hearted people are left!
I did not live life insisting on superiority.
Nor did I spend it chasing status, fortune or glory.

When alone with my thoughts, in solitude – solace, I find, only then.
Thousands of men, like us - thousands came, and thousands went.
There were poets forced to bend before authority,
There were poets, who kept silent, though they perceived everything,
Thousands of men, like us - thousands came, and thousands went.

Do not compare us to any of them.
On pedestals do not place us – as though we are majestic, mighty or big.
Any Kazakh who is able to write – is already a poet in his own right.
But is another Abay fated to arrive into this world?

You, the sensible youth!
My poems are like my friends with whom I share my secrets and truth.
But I find that a heart-to-heart does not suffice in quelling my passions.
What can a poet who's poured everything out possible hope to dream of?
Not one single thing in the cavernous depths of my heart lies stored…
***

***

Oh, the years …mirage-like you ebbed and flowed,
How you've exhausted me.
Those who must share the same fate as I,
Why have you vanished, where have you decided to hide?

Every day, you used to visit me,
We'd enjoy each other's company, amid the shade that cascaded down from the trees,
Ready to lay down your life for me.
Where are you now, older brothers, where am I to search for thee?

You, who used to keep me safe, away from the predator's claws,
My guardians, who always ensured that I was alright and well fed,
Gracefully gliding on the glassy canvas of water, like swans.
Where are you now, my tender-hearted Zhenge?

You who taught me to stand up for myself, be tough,
You hadn't grabbed the reins from my hands, you never bothered.
You who raised me, tenderly tickled my head with your scruff,
Where are now, my grandfathers?

Those who looked upon my unusual destiny,
Who looked after me, wiping their own tears,
To where have you gone, this place with no return?
Not just my own mother, but all of my Mothers…

Oh many years have gone by, many days,
Not even a question in my direction, no: "How are you?"
Where have you flown away to?
My majestic fawns, the mountains with your presence is full.

Come, settle down and surround me,
And I will pierce the air with my screams,
"Oh where, oh, where are you?"
Where are you my peers, my mentors, my comrades in destiny?
***

ONE-ROOM SHACK

The shack in which I grew up is but one pitiful room,
This room of mine, with its four-wall world.
Here I could do anything my heart wished to,
All those days, so many years ago,

The shack in which I grew up – but one pitiful room,
Back then, that one room could have been a thousand to me,
Offer me the great Khan's throne instead – and guess what?
I still wouldn't take it.

With my guests I would bid farewell to the sun,
And with my guests I would greet the dawn again,
And my grandma's white handkerchief always laying around,
Comforted me, beckoning without a sound.

The shack in which I grew up – just one pitiful room,
Everyone in its womb could find comfort – what a boon!
And this young man, having mounted his horse,
Hadn't bothered to ask me to step into his house.
Well, so it must be then, only God can truly judge him.
In fact, we bore witness to much worse things than this,
For we are a people with hearts open wide.
Hey there, chap, is there something about me that's not to your liking?

And why, oh, why did I ever sell
My childhood home? Now I certainly regret it.
I'm terribly sorry, chap, I retract it.
What happened to me so suddenly, what is this?
For it was I who was the gleaming hope of this household.
Hey there chap, if it's alright with you,
Please fetch me a cup of water, could you?

You're not one of those youths with no respect for their Elders, are you?
Do I really look like one who is not capable of being grateful?
Hey there, brother, hand me cup of water.
I'm asking you, please, can you hand it to me – this thirst – is oh, such torture!

BY THE CRADLE

Everywhere in the world, the silence is so similar,
Like the sweet face of a peaceful, tiny newborn.
Don't you dare wake him! Don't think you can touch
The cradle to swing my sleeping son.

Sleep, little child, sleep sweetly, I'm right here, you just sleep.
I need nothing from you, world. I have all of my treasures right here.
To me – all of my happiness, all of my wealth rests
In those precious moments when we embrace, and you hang from my neck,

Your tiny little giggles give my soul such shivers of joy!
I can't help but admire how you throat makes these little bubbles and ripples,
What is it, tiny light of my life, you're trying to tell me with these pouted lips?
My tender sweet, your babbling my heart does endlessly tickle.

What kind of mother could give birth to a person,
Who to an infant's sleep could be averse?
Oh, silence! Silence, is such utter bliss!
Such bliss it is when, instead of crying – your child just sweetly clings.

Everywhere in the world, the silence is so similar,
Like the sweet face of a peaceful, tiny newborn.
Don't you dare wake him! Don't think you can touch
The cradle to swing my sleeping son.

***

- We were children, weren't we?
- Indeed, just yesterday, we were children.

And how many winters have passed… and how many falls?

Now, children call us fathers,

Now, children call us mothers.

You were the boy who was always barefoot, perpetually chasing baby goats,

Perpetually threw stones through window-panes.

My sons, to you – I am grateful, for me you've done a good deed.

From your old man you've taken away all of his mischief.

Tell me, what's this silver dew that's changed your hair's hue?

Perhaps your wife tripped and happened to spill some flour all over you?

I'm truly amazed how you cope with the fact that it isn't the same.

Remember how you cried when you lost the knucklebone game?

- We were children, weren't we?
- Indeed, just yesterday.

It was noon-time.

(Seems that life hasn't taught you so much…)

Hey, quit looking at my head, maybe it's grey, but it's still held high!

Didn't you know that the mountain's peaks are the first to see a snowfall's streaks?

You see, all of my mischief I bequeathed to my children,

My hands were tied, nothing to try, so away it was given.

Hey, you know I could say you haven't exactly become more stunning.

How can you open your mouth to say such a thing – how unbecoming!

Only your eyes have not forgotten how to smile.

Your chest, a tad stretched, like a canoe – seems ready to meet the cliff's face anytime now.

But who was the trickster who decided to mix

All of those snow white threads into your dark hair, so thick?

There are these clouds hovering above your lash line, looking like they mean business.

I wouldn't upset them, try not disturb them, otherwise we'll be mopping up rivers,

I think someone's sketched and chiseled all along your forehead,

The effect is a bit reminiscent of a seagull flapping madly. Is it possessed?

You were my little camel pet, with sparkling eyes that shone so brightly,

And I was your beloved colt, with my mane flapping wildly.

And now, all is gone,

For I became a father, and a mother you've become,

And there is a mystery which binds us, despite it all – a bond that remains unspoken.

***

***

If you want to be a friend to me,
Please dear sir, respect my friends first.
And perhaps your friend
Will come to respect my friend
If, of course, we are to be friends.
So why don't you befriend my friend,
And I will gladly befriend yours?
How many friends have you got - a lot?
What a wonderful person you must be!
Me? Oh, I haven't got many.
My friend, could you recommend for me a remedy?
Perhaps you can befriend your friends with me,
To them, you must introduce me!
In all honesty, I'd be ready to be your slave,
I have such a longing for friendship.
I long for it, passionately!
I would gladly perish,
Taking my friend's faults to the grave.
It'd be much better to perish in the home of your friend,
Than to be a powerful vizier in the court of a villain.

***

THE NARROW PATH

"Tracks are the mother of the road." - Kazakh Proverb

There is a narrow little path that runs around and hugs my house,

And in life, it seems – on of the hardest things was to find a way out onto it.

From the narrow path, you could access the road, only through the thickest brush, so thorny.

The road's bends and curves twist and turn, at the crossroads of my heart and my soul.

This narrow path saw how my father had left for the terribly bloody war,

This narrow path saw me carry my grandma's casket after her passing.

This narrow path bore witness to the aftermath of my young daughter's illness, then her death.

These prints – though invisible, are in no way extricable – like a monument, indestructible.

In the steppes there lay many roads, across the steppes and along the valleys.

Careful my son, try not to get lost – err on the side of caution.

On this narrow path my mother and I advanced, until she saw me off on the wide road.

These roads were like wrinkles whittled into my grandma's face before she passed away.

And so, I follow that narrow path, and if I fall – I rise again.

I'm searching for the road, I'm searching for it – I must go forth, always looking ahead!

Oh no, how many potholes, cracks and bumps!

But I will still follow that path – falling, rising, and falling again – but this time,

I'm determined.

MEETING

- You were a fiery soul, a heart – beautiful ablaze.
How do you fair, my little bride, how do you fair, these days?
Somehow that capricious youth has left you, too?
Oh, life…
Such a shame!

Your personality was fickle, like that of a wild *khulan*,
When we came to visit you, we made sure to approach with caution.
In no way could we display any resistance in front of you,
And, worse came to worst, we instantly flew the coop.

- There is nothing left of me from those olden days,
How do you fair, brother-in-law, how are you fairing these days?
Unable to make heads or tails of it, recklessly,
You had a fondness for playing with both water, and fire.

You were so stocky, so firmly built,
And where is he now, that man, so wonderfully strong, like a hammer?
Oh, life… what a shame!
Could it really be that all things past, are not to be remembered?

We each went our own separate ways, each with his own worries,
The string of our conversation remains frayed, unfinished.
The springtime sky, having heavily sighed,
Bursting far-away in thunderous utterance,
 - Oh, life!

KARASAZ

I am fortunate.
I was born in the arms of a prosperous, promising land.
Oh, my precious, unrivaled Karasaz,
With your undeniably sacred waters!

Your tiny streams and little brooks,
Pumping life through me, so necessary, like my veins and arteries.
Indeed, you are my monastery,
With your undeniably sacred waters!

In the spring, the ducks would fly by, circling, and geese would glide right in, landing in the rivers,
And, oh the cranes, just to gaze upon them, would have me so elated.
In all probability, I wouldn't have written, not even a single poem,
If I was not born of the great Karasaz - no, not for a moment!

For the first time I laid gaze, at a fairly ripe age,
At these verdant mountains that seemed to consume the entire horizon.
- There is a vast land that must lie beyond these mountains!
Long ago, said my grandma to me, but I had not believed her!

Oh, my Karasaz!
Is it you, who is my untold truth,
The joy, for which time and again, I kept on searching?
To whom and how am I to begin to describe your bountiful wonders?
If one brims ablaze with desire – with his own eyes he ought to come, laying his gaze upon her.

THE LOST PLATOON

- Do we still march?
- We march, we do.
- Will we die soon?
- We will, we will.
We march, we're lost in bad terrain,
We freeze, warm up, then freeze again.

We have no clue, no road, no aim.
The night is dark; we can't see much.
If a horse missteps, you plunge straight down
Into an abyss, our ready-made grave.

The sky and the mountains – a black shroud
Above us, monsters fly around.
We ride, hagridden and perplexed,
 We pray to dead, to our ancestors.
 Our dead-beat horses hardly move
From highest peak to deadly grove

The summer, raining cats and dogs.
Heat-lightning sparks and fades away.
We have been lowed, been belittled,
But days were good, and we were free then.

- Are we still here?
- We are, we are.
- Don't waste your time for empty talk.
  And go, and go.
- You want to shoot me, silent guide?
- Just wonder, where is end of it?
- Don't worry! Worst to worst – we die!
- But as of now, we alive!

THE WAR'S LAST SPRING

Is it true, that everything was painted green?
Mountain slopes were the greenest of green,
And the hilltops, and the valleys,
Were blooming in emerald green.
The war's last spring.
Upon the green mountain peaks,
Gentle light-green cloud rings, nestled in.
Everything 'round flooded with sunshine,
The war's last spring
Has spilled her silver light down, like wings.
And look, even the turquoise sky,
Even the sky, has bloomed and opened in front of our eyes.
Hanging, suspended above the mountains high,
And the sun, shining in the sky, like a birthmark, heavenly.
Hiding its delicate flowers, jealously,
Even the weed-grasses bloomed, anew.
The war's last spring.
The green, youthful shoots of the willow,
Cloak the forests, a green uniform.
But, no high-spirits did it bring with it.
Look there, see that small shack in the back of the village?
The war's last spring.

GRANDMA, YOUR CANDLE WON'T DIM

Your eyes so clear and bright, radiating light,
For your only son you waited, hoping he'd come home from the bloody front.
In this world, there is nothing more painful than waiting,
So the melancholy took you from us, in the end.

Your hearth's warmth won't ever dim, grandma.
I will praise and sing hymns for you.
It's a shame that beneath seven layers of earth,
My hymns won't reach down through to you.

To your sole son's letters, you'd already bid farewell,
You took off on that journey – one with no return, one with no end.
When victory, exalted, was flapping her joyful wings,
 I rejoiced, hoping somehow, perhaps your son home she would bring.

Your hearth's warmth won't ever dim, grandma.
I will sing praises and hymns in your name.
Perhaps your only son will return now?
I, like you, will sit here, and wait.

But, alas, dearest grandma, your sole son - he did not return.
How wretched and painful when a person vanishes, vanishes without a word.
If he is alive and well - he is roaming out there, somewhere,
And if in fact, he is dead, he'll be lying with you - in that eternal bed.

Your candles have not been snuffed out, grandma.
This song I dedicate to you.
Your spring has not dried up, grandma.
Your sycamore tree stands tall, strongly bursting through.

For thirty years, I've watched the dawns of the morning,
Its cheerful rays it gifts to the world.
The song which your sole son, in melancholy, sang to you,
Is carried off swiftly by the swans now, their wings raise it up to you.

Your candle's flame won't wane, grandma.
This song I dedicate to you.
With your talisman still swinging round his neck,
Your sole falcon, graceful, flies high - ever beautiful.
Grandma, the flame of your candle, will not ever wane.

CHARACTER

What wonderful days, lately, I greet now!

Though, there was a time when my virtues, to you, did not appeal.

There was no purpose for us to have met now,

For, away to the place with return, far away to that place, I steal.

Into my soul you've embedded - such a terrible pain,

Oh my dearest, my beloved, how to you, this, shall I portray?

Am I to, again, ignite this old flame?

I want to repeat it over, repeat it over again.

In my soul, everything is abloom anew,

The swans have flown, and the lake's mirror surface – is transparent once more.

Has the north been met, by the warm southern wind?

The balmy breath from your direction, my face did greet, gently,

To meet its tender breeze, my face, in one spot, I gladly set.

I only hope, oh I hope it won't chill.

The cold must not get to it. I hope the freezing cold never will!

Even if your heart freezes, into an icy brick - I'll make sure to heat it.

Oh, why were you not born a bit later, a tad bit later than I?

Why was I not born earlier, not born earlier – why, oh why?

KHAN TENGRI – SKY KING

I do not acknowledge low-lying mountains.

Even a hill with a low mountain could bicker,

Who, to Khan Tengri, could ever compare?

Like the spear of my country, topped with brushes of mares,

The height of its peak - a great deal I adore,

And the sun, showering down from its heights, administers kisses to it.

Well, go ahead, tell me – who could boast of being mightier than Khan Tengri,

Who, with his shoulders, props up the sky, in its entirety?

If you have but one little sliver of the great Tengri's vigor,

Try to not get in his away, step away, away, quicker!

In the distance, stands an isthmus, from whose middle rises the great Kahn Tengri,

Like the great, milk-bearing chest on Tyan-Shan.

Even the sun, swirls around in a daze, and lays right at his feet,

And grey-silken mist surrounds him, shielding him in her deep.

In the chest of Khan-Tengri,

Is the deepest empathy and love for all of this earth.

Standing tall and firm, pointing up to the sky, his gaze he lays upon the valleys and hills,

The Sun – his mistress, the Sky – his home, and the Moon – his pigeon.

I have no liking for low-lying mountains,

They leave no traces in my soul,

I love the majesty that flows through nature,

To love the mightiest – that is my goal.

THE WANDERING GULL

My little one, where have you come from – my white, wandering gull?
Do not consider this place foreign, since you've already come.
Much grass and water you'll find in this valley, limitless,
Which has been the home and defender, of many mighty heroes and kings.
Its beginnings – defenseless, tender-necked, then with sable-wings,
You flew by me, and spying me - perhaps you considered me kin?
Should I shower upon you, from my hand, the gathered rays of the sun?
For it was you, who flew in with pure intentions,
I have no mirror surfaces for you to twirl you lacy traces,
It lulls you gently, my bare, naked steppe.
You couldn't touch down, my little fickle one, upon these piddling waves,
It is, truly, a pity – no waves exist in the pitch-black lake.
Who oppressed you so, little gull, upon you inflicted their will?
You've gotten lost, abandoned your dear Atirau, poor winged thing.
My little lakes and tiny springs – all of them, to you, I'm offering,
My downtrodden bird, wandering lost, with no Motherland.
Why upon this welcoming peak, have you not decided to land?
Ah, no waves there are for you, with whom, you can speak heart-to-heart,
In this life, anything you desire can be found,
Only the Motherland is given - but once.

***

When in a state of yearning - to my Motherland I'd returned.
I had always wondered – is someone missing me, from way back when?
Where are the fires of my village?
Could it be - they are no longer warm?
I grew up, frolicking, like a little yearling,
By the watering hole, my sloped banks of the river, so steep
I lived without any worries, utterly carefree
In the midst of these towering peaks,
In the midst of these pensive forests, dense with trees.
When in a state of yearning – to my Motherland, I'd returned,
Looking down from these radiant hills,
I'd think – is that my Zhenge tending to the kettle,
Wrapped in her yellow shawl, still?
And my grandpa , Sultanbai, could it be he's no longer alive?
And seeing him, with his grey beard, heavy and wide,
I felt rejuvenated, vivified.
I grew up, frolicking, like a yearling,
In my hills, bluffs and valleys,
I grew without worries, completely carefree
On this land, majestic and mighty,
Having carried with me the lessons life brings.
When, in a state of yearning, I'd returned, chasing my cherished dream,
I always wondered – will there be someone to come and greet me?
My head I bow, before these mountains,
Before the forests, my head, I bow.
There is nothing that I cherish more, nothing of which I'm more proud.

MY DEAREST ZHENGE

When I asked for water, you gave me both sweet and sour milk,
Oh, my dearest Zhenge, you've grown old quite quick!
Like a Jack of Spades from a deck of cards,
With eyes bulging from his face – who is this man, that stares at you, like this?

Why is his face so unkind, so stony and strange?
He looks upon everyone, scolding, his features imprinted with hate.
Like the stick of the highway police,
His little mustache spies on your every move, in wait.

Oh, my dearest Zhenge, do you remember my older brother?
We both respected him so, and loved him.
Curse and damn, that bloody war.
Oh, my dearest Zhenge, how your life to shreds it has torn.

Where is your laughter, ringing like silver?
Why is your face so glum, like the sky's twilight?
You were so free-spirited, not to be tamed.
Who with their lasso, has roped you in - your spirit, maimed, so?

If it was your decision, it was rushed, it certainly seems,
Evidently, this was not for happiness, but a choice you forced out of grief.
You'd been a person who could distinguish, one who'd judged quite well.
Many had presented themselves to you, and you'd stepped all over their chests.

All the mountain-men looked upon you, their prides their jewel – they considered you.
Having pulled on your Saptoma boots,
You stepped over many, so merciless,
And certain ones, with those very same boots, you'd grind right into the earth.

Oh, my dearest Zhenge – indeed, you've grown old quick!
Before, grief would not have made you his victim, no – not like this!
From where did the sadness arrive, leaving you so listless?
Or, perhaps, my dearest Zhenge, there is something you miss,
Your youth, now long-faded, having perished in the war?

TO THE WOLF

Oh, you ravenous devil!

Your sharp fangs - like diamonds, your temper so wild,

You leave your traces, along the mountains, and valleys, blood spilled in your wake.

Having appeared and vanished again, you think you'll slip away from me, this time?

Just you wait. Soon you'll make friends with my saddle's straps round your chest.

When I'd taken my herd to the pastures and valleys to graze,

I remember how you, puffed up and ready, came, and took care of them.

Don't worry, I'll come vengefully, and we'll settle this.

I'll put a bullet in you, tie you to my saddle, and that will be that for you.

Between boulders and ravines, you seeded your bloody kills.

Your thirst is never filled; your fangs with blood always drip, freshly spilled.

No thrill is enough for you, the weak ones you beat and snapped with your will.

Not once did you allow for a moment of stillness – the time will come, I will end you.

You are a wild beast unlike any other.

My dogs don't want your bones, with their dripping saliva to smother.

I will rob and strip you of your coat, I won't think on it for a minute.

Your limp, skinless remains I'll drag through the dirt, and leave them, upon you, to scavenge.

Go ahead, roam your hills and valleys for now,

Drunk from your limitless crimson supply, take shelter and rest in the brush.

Having smeared the hills and valleys with blood,

I know the day will soon come, I will strap you lifeless, to my saddle.

***

I feel

That it is not others I fear, but myself.

My own eyes, I fear,

And my cracked, parched lips.

No horse, have I – to gallop away, nor wings – to take off with the wind.

Oh, dear God!

I want to give it up once and for all, just quit!

My head is pewter, my feet are lead.

Ten years have passed by, I hardly noticed.

How did you not feel it?

My soul feels it, though – it comprehends

That the past is in the past, never to return again.

I've hit something – looks like a dead end.

My eyes dimmed, the light has dwindled – perhaps, somewhere deep in my soul it exists.

I cannot cry, nor can I grin,

Oh, dear friend!

Please return to me my long-forgotten laughter, again!

I fear only myself,

For it was I who killed me.

I pray I do not lose my mind.

No peace do I find, my thoughts run wild.

Oh, my dear friend,

I beg you, find my laughter, and return it to me, again.

Now is the time

For me to live, and to laugh.

***

***

I am in love!
No, truly, I love this person!
Right now, I care not about myself! I hope all, with her, is well?
Oh, Heavens! She is so utterly cold and cruel!
Is her beating heart made of bronze?

I am in love.
Why would I try to hide this?
To me, every hair she twirls, is made of gold.
I pine for her so, I feel tormented.
Wounded, I grieve – I grieve, a man in love.

Soaring higher and higher still – to unimaginable heights,
My white-winged bird, have you flown towards the sun, never to return?
Am I really to remain like this, knowing no semblance of peace,
Roaming the vastness of this world, in search of you, infinitely?

I'm trying hard to suppress, this thirst for you, which within me rests,
I've lost all of my hope and faith, it's scattered all over the place.
It seems, that so it is meant to be – I'm meant to wander the face
Of this Earth, a man in love, for eternity.
***

***

May everything remain as it will, what will be, will be,
I know, that you are not meant to join my song with me.
It remains an unknown to me, where you soul still roams these days,
Though my soul is even further away, further away than your own.

I've been unable to discover where your soul still hovers,
You've probably found a new passion, some new hideaway.
Like rails, upon which train cars ride,
Different dreams on one pair of rails, certainly cannot align.

What will be, will be.
May everything remain
Just as it is.
For every person is like a forest, unique.
Walking into it freely - is easy, than to get lost within its depths,
Much simpler than to emerge from its thicket ever-dense, to find the road again.
***

A CONVERSATION WITH AYBAR

Yesterday, Aybar came to me, and made me feel somewhat ashamed:
- Father, how old were you at the time of the war?
- Ten years of age.
- So why did you not engage in combat with the others, defend your Motherland?
There were many war heroes I know of, who had only been ten.

- Back then, I was ten, only ten,
I was busy defending myself.
And the people defended me.
If the ten-year olds like me had not defended themselves,
There wouldn't be an inkling of a single Aybar around, like yourself,
Don't pick at my unhealed wounds, dear little friend.

Back then I was ten, only ten.
And though I did not fight, I had a difficult life.
That which my father for us had preserved and left,
With grandma, safely, everything I'd kept.
All, so that they would not die,
The other ten-year olds, that were stuck, fighting on the front.
I bashed the frozen dirt, so that we could plow it.
And so, this was the beginning of my poetic life!

My childhood was gone, swept away - carried by the wind,
It was not for us, to have tasted her honey or sugar.
If ten-year-olds had not learned to defend themselves,
They could not stand in defense of others, my son!

TO MY LIFE

I thought you would be brief,
Like a brief, brief poem.
But you've grown quite long, oh, life of mine.
I thought
You'd be a mischievous son,
But you've grown into a daughter, to walk to the altar,
Dearest life of mine.
I thought that you – were lightning,
Flashing in the dark blue sky,
Yet, I am – a teardrop,
Glistening in dark, dark eyes.
Why did you compare me, to the life of a somber raven?
Do I appear to be one?
Who will always have grains and foods in abundance?
Oh, life of mine,
I don't understand you much.
I can't seem to understand you!

***

You – are the eyes of our ancestors?

You – are the words whispered by the lips of our wise men?

You – are the essence of our rattled hearts,

Created simply to feel?

Oh, my Dombyrah!

You are my dark-grey duckling, my lovely snow-white swan!

You are my dream, my sorrow, my secret, my tomorrow!

***

PUSHKIN, FAREWELL

"We are birds, flying free – it is time, brother, it is time..."
"Prisoner", Pushkin.

Well, let us bid farewell, then, brother of mine, my guiding star.
Tomorrow, I will fly away to my free, immeasurable steppe,
With the piercing gaze of an eagle – in the vastness of the steppe,
With the agility of an eagle – up in the mountains, high.
Tomorrow, I will fly away, into the vast flatlands, of my beloved steppe.

For now, brother of mine, let us bid farewell, farewell, oh, guiding star.
Do not blame, do not blame your dear brother.
The poet's strength - lies not in acclaim,
The poet's strength – lies in his moral composure.

I want to tell you, beloved older brother,
My heart has grown sour, and with various pleasures, I don't even bother.
A fool, sometimes – my conscience,
With hands, which I dirty - again and again.

The time in which you lived – is a haze; it has faded from me.
Yet, somehow, no mercy did the cursed century attempt to shed on us still.
Thinking, perhaps, come alive, Pushkin's iron statue will decide to walk away.
So, your pedestal, they bound round in many a steel chain.
I looked upon your sculpture of bronze,
Even bronze, I could comprehend.
God created me to admire and bow.
No right have I to go down – only up, up, again.

I found myself amidst festivities, a crowd immersed in celebrations joyful.
I got rather drunk, rather full of immodesty – chest puffed, so prideful.
I came here, to part with all of my grief. "Fly away!" you said to me,
And since you told me to "fly," I soared straight up into the sky.

To the mountains I'd flown, creamy clouds their majesty did enrobe,
And the sky then tilted, spilling its azure milk upon the stillness of sea.
Having snatched the calm from the sea and the atmosphere,
The furious storm, without warning, with it in its clutches, did retreat.
Farewell, beloved older brother, this world you certainly did captivate.
Into the chest of the "Marble Guest", with your living soul, you crept.
There is no other wind quite like it, that will enjoy such freedom as this,
My Alatau, my towering mountains, we will meet. Yes, we will meet soon!

ON TRUTH

From olden times, Truth throws its gaze upon you – eye to eye.

Your soul cannot escape Truth's judgment, it's but a pesky little fly.

And when the verdict is read by dignity and truth,

Into their grip will slither untamed shrews.

Their grips will also clutch the likes of tricksters and villains and such,

And charlatans, and frauds, and swindlers, too - all who deceive to their benefit.

The fiery blade of Truth shall not ever cool

Until it has annihilated, consumed, ev'ry single thief and scoundrel, too.

For some, the Truth is like a shroud.

By it, they are bound – using it, as a shield of protection.

But if Truth were to come, and tear down this curtain,

Like a pesky fly, the soul would take cover, and hide, the pitiful thing - deep, deep in the earth.

***

That, over there – is the sky, and this here – is my garden.
Look, the sky is full of clouds, and my garden is tired and wilted.
The downy fluff flies through the air, oh, so slowly,
Oh, look, now winter has decided to show up.

In the distance between the sky and earth,
Wise-Man Winter's arrived to administer healing.
The wounds of Nature,
He tends to patiently, each injury bandages, tediously.

With gauze wrappings veiling their heads,
They call out, begging to be dressed again,
Wandering in the gardens, the Willow and the Birch,
Barefoot, they mournfully weep.

Bare branches hugging its bulk,
The Elderly Oak frowns with furrowed brows.
Winter – is pure, Winter – is innocent, pure, and clean.
A time to repent, winter is poetry,
***

MY GOAL

I do not write poems.
I speak heart-to-heart with the soul.
My sorrows I share with those living presently, indeed – they all secrets hold.
In the wake of the this age, caught in a whirlwind of haste,
Step-by-step, I move with caution great.

I do not desire to write poems,
Weaving each line with the next, utter care and diligence.
If they flow through me, effortlessly, or even stage a coup,
I won't glue them together, nor bind their feet with concrete.

But, if like a little devilish imp, it suddenly springs on me,
A poem is born, and to it, I do not return.
Staining the delicate sky,
I shall speak with the bitter tongue of Truth, each time.

In my soul, the flame will always blaze,
I do not cease the art of self-exploration. Of this, I never tire.
Oh, my heart!
Do not tremble, keep still,
Do not permit these treacherous lies to tiptoe closer.

When I cry: "I",
It is actually, not I – at all.
Don't worry, I won't try to convince you.
May the unbelievers bathe in their lack of belief,
In order to grasp someone's soul and within it, the core- it's secret,
I am certain, that one must first start - by looking inward.

Everything that rests within me,
Rests within you, and him, too.
So then, whatever is "Mine" that is within you,
Will remain with you,' til the end.
First, you must unfold, then slowly unravel your soul,
This will be the greatest blessing.

I do not see the purpose in announcing my love for each person,
It is a bribe, this heady declaration.
I, too, love each of you,
But, you will never hear me say it.
Left alone, in solitude, I feel that burning, and buzzing yearning inside my chest.

Everything in my chest is up in flames.
This is why I am filled with such sorrow.
I will hide this from you, to write poetry is often amusing.
But to embody poetry,
Is such a heavy weight on the soul!

MY AGE

He protected me, like a costly gem, enveloping me in his shelter.
This life, this time – is so precious to me.
In all probability, this age – is embedded within me.
I listen to its every gentle breath, trembling.
This age, ticks like the clock within my heart,
It seems each tick is completely in sync.
If, by chance, I happen to doze off,
My age, seems to doze off right along with me.
This is my time, this is my age,
Each fleeting moment – a luxury.
If your age wanders off into that distant realm,
How can you possibly stay still, and not follow it?
Tirelessly, I always heed the wise advice of my trusted friend,
Listen closely to his every breath.
What secrets has he kept from me?
It seems our generation will have a tough go of it
To bid this age farewell, in to the murky unknown.
Will our generation have to bear witness to this?
The ages – they come and they go, oh, they come and they go.
I will sing the praises for this age,
And the future generations will sing of it differently, in their own special ways.

MY ANCESTORS, MANY THANKS TO YOU

Oh, my ancestors – a great many thanks to you!
When I came into this life blind, deaf and mute,
Alongside my musical instrument, you gifted me with songs and speech,
May your children not grow up bound and ignorant.
My beloved ancestors – a great many thanks to you!

The songs that by bards are yet to be writ,
The secrets yet to be uncovered of princesses,
The woeful tears and grief,
Carried to me the sounds of the deep.

Your lifeless, barren steppe,
What have we not survived, seen or wept through, my sacred land?
The lines that are yet to be writ of my history,
I found buried in the betrayals of your utterances.

I know not,
Perhaps, back then, this joy drifted down to land upon you.
You erected cities grand, smashing the gardens of paradise to bits.
The signs, chiseled in to the stony cliffs,
I bow to them, and listen to their words, wisdom-filled.

The lifeless, barren lands of the steppes do not reveal their secrets.
Nor do the signs upon the stone cliffs, they do not reveal them to me.
Plucking at the strings of the dombyrah,
I chased after your mystery, your nature.

I ceaselessly searched for you, in moments of woe and sheer desperation,
Every time, going back to the signs, your legends chiseled in stone.
Every time, I rewound the clock back, I was born again, again coming to life:
Today, my history, I've decided to write,
My dearest ancestors, I write them in your mother tongue!

This is the day I was born again.
Speak to me, orchestra, loudly ring, louder, thundering!
Speak to me, Mozart, in my mother tongue,
Speak to me, Dante, in my mother tongue!

I WANT TO BE LIKE MOUNTAINS

The mountains were given to me to keep me amongst the living.

If I release a heavy sigh, the mountains weep loudly in reply.

If a whirlwind swirls within my heart,

The mountains respond with blizzard of billowing snow.

The mountains lowered their passes for me, easing the crossing of rivers.

Unravelling their dale and valleys, a verdant display – just for me, they put on this show.

And so, you've grown, the mountains your own mighty cradle.

Oh, life of mine, how you never cease to amaze me!

Lulled by the mountains embraces,

You grew in the cool shades of tall fir trees.

Oh, destiny, will you, finally abandon

All of your woes and misery, which empty your soul till it's barren?

Or will you, yet again, unravel them?

The majesty of these mountains – this is my allotment,

My joy and my grief, in their own ways unique.

The Elders always said to me: "Be like the Mountains, tall!"

I want to be like Mountains – stand tall, with the highest peaks!

TO MY MUSE

Come, admire my glum, sour mood.

Where, oh where have you gone to?

Oh, Muse! I liken you to a swirling whirlwind.

If I open my mouth, into my lungs you thrust and howl your gusts,

As though we happened upon an abandoned windmill.

Chilling my soul, strung up in the cold,

The wind howls, my chest like bellows of a blacksmith.

Why have I arrived at such gloom?

Oh, Muse!

Where have you gone to, my flowing source of inspiration?

Giving free reign only to the fire and its flames,

Where are you, my trusted companion?

My notebook lies, untouched, on the table.

Is it destined to be left like this - pitiful, never to be filled full?

My thoughts hover around me, not allowing me to uncover these clouds of gloom.

I feel as though I'm crushed by a multi-ton, leaden balloon.

Oh, Muse!

How you've tormented me! Why must I suffer like this?

Bring me some hope and some strength.

And if it's not too much to ask, gift me with height and with depth,

Oh, my wonderful Muse!

Bless me for the long journey, ahead!

In front of me, do appear. I'm in need of your support.

OH, HOW SHAMEFUL

First, you left.
Then, I left after you.
After that, he decided to leave the village, too.
We should be ashamed of ourselves,
A shame to the beloved people of our aul.
Oh, how shameful,
Yes, so shameful,
So shameful, brothers of mine!

We were the hope of our humble people.
How are we to look them in the eyes?
We were the sole hope of all those who fought on the bloody front.
We were the only ones they had left behind.
And somehow, we still decided to leave.
To you, we turned the other cheek.

Do you hear it? Listen, listen well
To the cool breeze drifting in from the passes. Do you hear it whispers, gentle?
This is the sign of affection and welcome,
To you, to me, to him,
Telegraph wires that hang from wooden poles.

You will be able to see soon,
How to us, the high mountain peaks are waving,
The Elders with their silver-white beards,
With their pan-pipes fashioned from reeds,
Reminding you of the birds, who surely have returned,
Tweeting out beautiful songs, our native melodies.

Such a long time they waited for us.
Their eyes have dimmed, their sight has grown weak.
The sun seemed burnt, as it did when it set.
Such a long time they awaited us.
The stars seemed to melt and streak across the sky.
Even the graves,
It seemed, did weep for us.

Were the sole hope
Of a humble village people
Who saw support and strength in us.
We searched for joy away from our people.
We built separate lives apart from our village, ourselves we distanced.
When is enough, enough?
Get on your knees, now, in the great Motherland's earthen dust!

THE MOON – IN THE SKY, AND I – ON THE EARTH

I am alone,
And the moon in the sky is, too.
That fascinating wonder,
Is everyone eavesdropping on us?
I am – on the Earth. The Moon – is high in the sky,
Just the two of us,
We talk, without speaking a single word.

You were my unreachable dream,
And your rays you merrily spilled down for each any everything.
When you peeked through the grey shroud of the clouds,
Having hidden from sight, with your beautiful rays I did play.
Like a massive balloon, you'd rise in the East,
You truly must be a goddess, I thought to myself.

Wait, I've something to tell you – please don't hide yet,
You - whom I prayed to, you - who betrayed me.
You shine, but your glisten is cold now – it's bleak, almost morbid to me.
You seem to overflow with colors, but this is just for appearances.

Oh, you exquisite beauty, you are so foreign to me.
Is it possible, for a beauty to be filled with so much misery?
I see, you are no goddess, after all.
Instead of praying to you, I'll think I'll stick to praying to me.

***

Where are my steeds, my pastures, and where is my village, too?

Where are you dear mountains? Tell me you haven't changed!

From the grasslands, right up to the front door of the house,

Would baby goats and roe-deer, frightened and jumpy, still be found?

The wandering clouds, greet each other as they meet up there in the sky,

Do they still consult with each other, when they take their occasional breathers up high?

It seems they have no desire to leave my village, after all.

The sky, forever high, the earth and water, too – you were always my true friend till the end.

My head is full of so many lingering thoughts; I'm so cheerful when I'm around you.

All that perishes, and all that is born, resides within your chest.

The tall sky, and the watery-earth, if you live endlessly, that would be best.

The sun I trust. I will gladly bow to you, and the earth – you, I trust, too.

If I happen upon a handful of seeds, I will happily sow them in you.

If to this earth, the world shows no mercy,

Then not into earth, but into ashes I yearn to turn.

Upon this earth I grew, and as I always had before, in the Earth I will trust till I'm through!

***

THE GUARD

If you are going to pay Murat a visit,
Don't wait for him to ask. Say straightaway - "All is calm."
- Ah, but is stillness, my children, truly peace and quiet?
While warming himself in the sun, he would ask this, all summer and winter long.

He, too, knows winters – filled with nothing but ice and dimness.
He knows all – the warm nights, and the warm greetings of the dawn.
He knows the kind of life, that can make us young and strong,
The life of my country, freed of all things that make us worry.

The war, which the heart – left cracked and scarred,
In that old chest of his burns, then freezes hard.
Four sons he sacrificed for this peace and stillness,
Four brides-to-be to foreign grooms he had given.

The four brides-to-be bore him grandsons, four,
He, their supporter, and they – his protectors.
In summing up his life, everything evened out in the end.
"I started off with four swarthy men, and ended up with four little ones instead."

Now, the old man stands, a strong tall poplar – surrounded by young little shoots.
Forget about eighty, he plans to live well past a hundred.
In response to words of greeting:
"Is all calm?" he always asks.

To both young and old, who are flustered, always bustling about,
He gazes upon them, "Is all calm?" he warily asks.
When thunder booms through the sky, and lightning cracks its bright whip,
He gazes upon the sky, "Is all still?" he warily asks.

In life there are many dangerous pitfalls,
The old man has chosen to be the guard who never sleeps.
He feels, that if he were to ever doze off, even for a little bit,
His four beloved grandsons might vanish, into various parts of the deep.

***

She'd taken the jug,
To fetch the water.
I pine away for my young, lovely queen.
In her ear, a little ring did gleam.
I chased after my dream,
For my little colt, I am still yearning.

Digging for roots,
And for berries, too -
My dense forests, I pine for you.
The ducks on the water would land,
Into the glass-like surface, tracing their wingspan.
My lakes, how I yearn for you.

The herd is well-fed again,
And they doze off, blissfully,
It is this stillness and peace, I also miss.
Blowing me soft kisses,
And then stealing off into the distance,
I long for you, my mountain wind!

I lived so carefree,
No worries, nothing of which to speak,
I long for my youth, so naïve.
She used to say, "You are mine."
She used to tell me, "You rouse me."
I pine for her pure and radiant eyes.
***

BRIDES-TO-BE

When thunder roared suddenly through the sky,
One got word of her husband's death.
The other's vanished without a trace.
They never even came to lay him to rest.

The third one's husband returned,
Minus an arm, and minus a leg.
(He was fined the cheapest price to cheat death).
At least a heart still beats within his chest.

The fourth one, whose husband returned in one piece,
Returned, healthy, to a life of stillness and peace,
Whenever she sees one of the widows,
Weeps with more grief, than the widow herself.

Each one knows the other's secrets,
From each other, no secrets they keep.
And much like in their youth,
Every morning, each other, they greet.

Deep in their souls, their secrets are kept,
These four brides, the closest of friends,
Need not say a word, all is known, even silently,
Each preserving the other's dignity.

I write poems,
But who needs them?
I seek to heal the wounds of my scarred soul.
I am like Medjenuhn, ambling about, all alone,
Each day, further and further away from reasonable people.

I write poems.
I don't know what these writings will bring.
I witness only death around me, instead of flowering.
The grief of the people, and their bliss,
I thought I'd sing the only way I'm able.

What good can the woebegone honesties of a hopeless man bring
The revelations of a man, who on a daily basis, with himself, is fighting?
Rousing, stirring my thoughts, one day I decided to chase after my dreams,
And I embarked on what I call – the Path of No Return.

Embarking on the path of no return,
Now I will not turn back, no - not even a glance.
I write poems; all that I've longed to say, having said, I'll meet my end,
Even if I'm to stand, facing the gallows.

www.ingramcontent.com/pod-product-compliance
Lightning Source LLC
Chambersburg PA
CBHW031255230426
43670CB00005B/196